Tough Men Don't Cry

by

Daniel Wirth

Tough Men Don't Cry

Published by Empty After Publishing

United States of America

ISBN 979-8-9954139-0-5

9

Table of Contents

4.

Dead Weight

5.

Burning Bones

Epilogue

Folded Laundry

Ready

Foreword

By My Father, Harald Wirth

Men's emotional health continues to be one of the most quietly neglected areas of well-being in modern society. We talk endlessly about physical fitness, gym routines, nutrition plans, annual check-ups and step goals. But the inner landscape of feelings, fears, grief, shame, loneliness, and quiet desperation often remains invisible, or worse, dismissed as something men should simply "handle."

The truth is that emotional health is not secondary to physical health; it is every bit as foundational. When it erodes, it quietly undermines sleep, concentration, relationships, physical vitality, decision-making, and even the immune system itself.

Societal scripts handed down for generations still whisper (and sometimes shout) the same old rules to boys and men: "Be strong." "Don't cry." "Tough it out." "Real men don't complain." "Man up." These aren't clichés, they form a powerful, invisible cage. Admitting vulnerability can feel like breaking an unspoken contract, like betraying an identity that was carefully constructed from childhood onward. The result is predictable: many men learn to bury pain rather than name it, to perform composure instead of feeling it, to isolate rather than reach out. Over time that suppression builds pressure and results in chronic stress. Anxiety shows up as irritability or numbness, depression disguised as exhaustion or cynicism, and in the most serious cases, substance use or thoughts of self-harm as desperate escape valves.

Among all the sources of emotional strain men carry, few cut as deeply or consistently as distress that originates in human relationships. It isn't only romantic heartbreak or divorce, although those are undeniably brutal. It's also the slow fracture of long friendships that drift apart without explanation, the sting of betrayal by someone once trusted, the constant low-grade tension of feeling unseen or undervalued at work, the unspoken rivalry or comparison with colleagues, the guilt of not being the father/brother/son/partner others expect, the loneliness that creeps in even when surrounded by people. Relational wounds often hurt the most because they strike at our deepest need to belong, to be known, and to matter to others. And unlike a broken bone or a virus, these injuries are invisible to everyone else and the man suffering them usually suffers in silence, convinced that voicing the pain would make him weak, burdensome, or "less than."

For much of my own life I embodied exactly that pattern. I became an expert at taking emotional hits without flinching on the outside. Conflict at home, disappointment from friends, professional setbacks, parenting worries, financial pressure, the thousand small rejections and misunderstandings that make up daily life. I absorbed them all quietly. I could appear calm, steady, even helpful in the moment; people often described me as "level-headed" or "the rock." But in the private hours, late at night, during long drives, in the shower, lying awake beside someone who had no idea how much I was carrying, the worry churned. I replayed conversations, searched for what I could have said or done differently, tried to logic my way out of feelings that refused to be solved like a math problem. I internalized the belief that showing the strain would make things worse: it would worry my partner, disappoint my kids, erode respect at work, confirm that I wasn't as strong as I was supposed to be.

That way of being came with a high cost, even if it took years to fully recognize it. Eventually I began to see how much of my inner life I had walled off. Not just from others, but from myself. And I decided I didn't want to pass the same blueprint on to my children. So I made a deliberate shift: I started encouraging them, from a young age, to name what they were feeling. Not to fix it immediately, not to perform toughness, not to minimize it with "it's not a big deal," just to say it out loud. "I feel angry." "I feel left out." "I'm scared this might happen." "I miss you." Those small permissions became doorways. When they saw that naming emotion didn't shatter anything, that it often made things lighter, clearer, more connected. They began to trust the practice. And slowly, I started trusting it more myself.

Expressing what lives inside us is not a luxury or a sign of fragility; it is one of the most effective ways we have to interrupt the cycles of isolation, shame, and silent suffering. When a man risks saying "This hurts" or "I feel lost right now" or "I'm angrier than I know what to do with," something important happens: the weight gets distributed. The emotion stops ricocheting endlessly inside one skull and enters the shared human space where it can be witnessed, met, sometimes held. Very often, that act of honest naming gives permission to others in the room to lower their own armor. Vulnerability is contagious in the best way. It normalizes the truth that everyone is carrying something.

That's precisely the space Daniel is trying to open through his poetry.

He doesn't write polished, flowery verse meant to impress or decorate. His poems are deliberately raw and unfiltered, direct, sometimes jagged around the edges. They name anger without apology, loneliness without euphemism, confusion without pretending to have it all figured out. There's no posturing, no attempt to sound "poetic" in the conventional sense. Instead there is something far rarer: genuine emotion placed on the page exactly as it arrived, unvarnished and unashamed. In a culture that still trains men to hide the messy parts of being human, that kind of forthrightness becomes quietly radical. It says, without ever needing to preach: You don't have to perform invincibility to be worthy of being heard. You don't have to solve your pain before you're allowed to feel it. And you're not alone in carrying it.

If even one man reads those lines and feels a little less like he has to keep everything locked away, if one person recognizes their own buried ache in someone else's words and thinks, "Maybe it's okay to say this out loud," then the work has already done something quietly powerful.

From a very proud father.

Harald

Preface

How does one navigate the emotional ride of life? We are oftentimes thrown into a world where our emotions are obstacles and must be avoided at all cost.

Silence is interpreted as strength and stoicism as wisdom.

But we are deeply emotional beings at heart and need to express ourselves in a trusting manner.

This book was written for those moments when we pretend we are "fine."

It will take you on a journey from protective behavior through the cracks in our thoughts and the decay of holding it in, to the transformation and connection we make through empathy.

These poems reflect many stages of emotional trauma that we all experience, but rarely voice.

This is a mirror that shows you your reflection and builds on it with shared experiences.

This book is for those who carry responsibility in silence. Those who struggle to express their emotions and anyone who feels alone in their strength.

Strength and vulnerability can exist in us at the same time. We can be emotionally mature and professional.

It truly matters that we listen to our inner self and get a deeper understanding of our emotional map.

We are not alone on this journey, if these words can help you connect to others on a deeper level, then we can create a better world together.

1.

The Armor We Wear

Full Body Armor

Each word was a blow from the hammer

that shaped this armor

The pain we endured drove the flames

The oil we cried

black and thick

treated this metal

We singed our hair on the furnace

of Life

But blisters won't stop us

We carry our scars with pride

They are a warning to our enemies

Called to Duty

We are called to duty
in many ways
We respond in one
Yes sir/ma'am

And so we serve
We give everything
and get nothing
And that's fine

Utility

We needed love once
Our strength now comes
from being utility
We isolate in between

Guarding our solitude
we forge armor
becoming blacksmiths
Iron and fire loves us

We can shape safety
and death

Chestplate

I carry my strength on my chest
It's the first thing you see
It's a badge given to me
and i was never asked if i wanted it

I can't handle everything

I struggle with many things

Is nature ever wrong?
or do we humans just tend to
accept extremes
and call them our own.

Statistics

The wrongdoings are our own

Now statistics

for what not to do

what not to say

We need a map for navigating

the emotions around us

Emotions we turn into

Armor

to hide behind

Borders for others

Corrupted

Success is Armor

We pay with sanity
but can only afford thin metal

Covered in insecurities
we inhabit bodies destined
to fail

Walls of Flesh

Unbreakable we stand
The ground under our feet
Shall give before we do
A wall of blood and flesh

None shall penetrate this armor
For it is built with willpower
Without this armor
We become soft

So we wear it day and night
The weight can be crushing
But strength is made from struggle
So we struggle

Castles made of Sand

As independent men we
Grab the world
And mold our castles
Made of sand

We don't depend on others
Our walls are strong
They hold our front lines
From our enemies and our brothers

Our loneliness guarded behind safety
Passage is forbidden through locked gates
Now we see isolated sunsets
That only touch our eroded castles

Brick Heart

My heart is red
made of brick
To prevent cracking I make sure
to always redo the mortar

but this feels so heavy in my chest

And I can't let anyone in
because i forgot
to install a door

I Said I am Fine!

I am not Fine

I struggle to feel

Every day I lie to myself

That it will get better

And the darkness just remains

I see faint lights

But am chained to this block

So the lights go out

I sit with myself

Wishing I could break these chains and

Accept the light

But I have no strength

2.

The Fractures

My Voice Breaks

You know the feeling

when your chest tries to fold in on itself

It wants to consume its center

then the tight feeling gets stronger

But you fight it and

quietly whisper

I Love You too

In Debt

I owe a lot

Many times have i upset others

Many times was i in the wrong

But weakness = giving in

So my account is in debt

And here it goes

I am sorry

I am sorry for the times i ignored you

for the times I let you down

for the times I made you feel horrible

Shards

I drop another plate on the tile
The shards run across the floor

How I would like to tear myself
Into a thousand pieces
like that plate
and have them all run
in different directions

But in one piece I remain
and pick up the shards

Addicted

I fill my days with headphones
with artificial worlds
with unfamiliar voices

I am an addict
feed me anything but
stillness

Make this time run faster
I can end it now
but that's cheating

Scalded Anger

I burn myself on the fresh brew
but the pain fades
under the safety
of my anger

My emotions don't ask questions
They protect
from evil and good alike

A fighting style i learned young
to survive the lion's den

Great, now i have blisters on my tongue

Factory Reset

I dive deeper into my main frame

There has to be a switch here somewhere

I need to reboot

Last night i shut down

It was impossible

to know what i was feeling

so i faltered

An abrupt shutdown

No saved data

No easy ending

Now back to factory reset

Burnout

When the sun rises I wake up
exhausted from sleeping
My rest consists of coffee
and quiet car drives

I torture myself through the day
just to fall
through the mattress
into the next day

I grab my coffee and
go on the attack

Falling Behind

Time just melts in our hands
flowing through our fingers
dripping onto the floor
Barefooted we stand
in a puddle of the past

It needs to stand still for a while
so we can catch up
Finally live out our childhood
but this we are denied

And so forward we go
staying behind

Trembling Hands

One look at my hands
and I see that this life is unsavable
but we try anyways right?

I have failed so many times
please let me not fail again
My blood soaked hands
shake uncontrollably

And I accept defeat
Now where is the bathroom

Loneliness

The silence echoes louder
now that everyone left

You stand at the edge
looking back
at a life torn apart
the fibers dancing in the wind

There used to be ground beneath your feet
but earthquakes collapsed the cliffs
into the ocean
and now you fall forever

3.

Rust

Unforgotten

I am scared of fading

Slowly dissolving into

Nothing

Forgotten

We want witnesses

People who know

we existed once

Rust

dissolves metal

The red of a sunset

ends the day

Dust to Dust

Disintegration
is our inevitable outcome
The flaking of skin
like rusting metal

A red death from
simply sitting in the rain
for way
too
long

Injured Animals

After the fall
we limp into the old forest
where we can heal
Fragility dethrones us

Unseen and unheard
We sit on our competence
This will go over in silence

Honor
Strength
Nobility
Intact

but the fractures split
a little more

Machine Minds

Now we erase our minds
and create a hull
a muscular machine
incapable of feeling

Numbness sets into our face
We focus on getting it done
As promised we move
with precision

Gold Rush

Another breath escapes
with force
Another muscle aches
Twitching

A blood filled vein
Mined for its protective gold
Once the gold rush begins
An endless supply is demanded

A man works
until the body
Or the mind
fails

So it has been

So it is

So it shall be

I’ll do it Tomorrow

Tomorrow

Later

On the 1st

The beginning of never

We erase our future

with promises we don't

intend to keep

reaching for the first excuse

to betray ourselves

And in the end

we become cowards

Aches and Pain

Every step loosens the corrosion
in my ankles

Cracking footsteps give away my
nightly voyage to the bathroom
My joints ache with burning desire
for a painless existence
but every day is filled
with self torture

A strong sense of dread
weighs my body down
into the ground

And rising back up
is signing my rights away

for a normal painless life

So we purchase

Aches and Pain

every day

Collecting dust

We lay more passions on this altar
to collect dust
Our identities still use these instruments
but our actions don't

So we sit
leaning against this altar
for decades we prayed to our passions
until we have to sneeze from
all the dust
and the past falls to the ground
and shatters

They were not important after all

The Table

Dinner feels like an interview
where no questions are asked
Silence stares into our minds
and stress elevates

We have nothing to say
A pairing of forgettable stories
that have all been told
So we sit in this silence

Fading Memories

Another number fades
My memory isn't what it was
I can feel the poison in my brain
A corrosive substance
absorbed over time

Often we forget what it felt like
to experience something new
now time passes faster
We don't need to hold onto
boring images

And if we want to
they fade anyways

4.

Dead Weight

Be Perfect

Eyes everywhere
Our actions are judged
by everyone
but ourselves

We respond with
obeying what is asked
A letdown of many
for perfection is improbable

Puppets

A world of deception

raising generations

of good little puppets

strings attached

Earn

Learn

Perform

Love is earned

a man gets paid for his work

Skills are learned

I can fix that

Perform

Be an actor

Act your age

Sweaty Hands

My hand slips

And you fall

This tower was higher

than we thought

This is my fault

Heavy Shadows

We are glued to our shadows
and they only show the smiles
we tried to hide
the kisses we didn't give

They absorb all the things
we don't want the world
to see

Shadows hide our fears
our desires
our weaknesses

They are the stone unturned
and hopefully they stay heavy

Running in Place

A man can erode away
like rock and stone
when the rivers of endurance
keep pushing

When acceptable becomes
unseen
we become part of a machine
no one knows how it was created

And onward it runs
unlike the man
who is chained to
stagnation

Soulless

We bring ourselves to judgment
locking up our freedom
As criminals we roam the world
with pain behind soulless eyes

We lost our souls in the battles
that lasted decades
They took everything from us
including ourselves

Hanged

|

|

|

|

|

A noose slips over our neck

We can't help but admire

The slipknot

What a piece of art

Corpses

A thick rope over the shoulder
the dead weight digs
deep into the soil

Muscles like a water buffalo
we pull the corpses of our insecurities
they are coming with us
as reminders

We keep going

We do this

We do it quiet

We do it in pain

We do it with fear

We do it tired

We do it sad

We do it broken

We do it

We do it

We do it

Always

Specialty Tools

We are utility
but we are the unused tools in the toolbox
Weight carried to every jobsite
and never used
So special that we become
useless
And until a hand reaches for us
we stay silent

A pipe wrench can be a hammer too
and a screwdriver can be a crowbar

Our utility shifts the more tools are lost
and eventually our time will come
When carrying our weight
will be worth it after all

5.

Burning Bones

Gravesite

Two feet stand
where you once stood
a grave of the old self
burried in the ground

You deserve broken bones
They are the honesty of
your physical limits
the pain endured

As warriors we stand
amongst the flowers
that live
where death lies

What makes You?

One more calculated move
can sharpen the blade
that is you
to be razor sharp

One more breath
can nock the arrow
that flies
True

One more unsaid word
can force the enemy
into making the mistake
that makes you

The Push

It starts in the fingers
when the hand holds
the better choice

It creeps into our legs
when our feet take us
down the hard road

It settles in our brain
We become resilient
in our pursuit

Controlled Breath

How can we rise
like flames
reaching for the heavens
with tentacles driven by heat

We need to grab the air
that boils our blood
and smash it on the floor
then inhale its poison

To fuel our future
ensure our survival
build the base of
our existence

Adrenaline

It burns with cold flames
blue fire Runs
through our skin
and we rely on the pain

To push us
To harden us
To burn us
Alive

We endure the necessary
with open arms
asking for more

Aim True

It's all hard
It's Torture
and it can remain
or torture can change

The tension will eventually give
Where it takes you
is up to your aim

Tending the Fire

We wake up with that burning in our chest
A call for action on procrastination

Imagine being pulled by a force
that changes the outcome of your future
Then you act on it
blindly following the instinct
that was bred into you
overcoming fear and anxiety

Because if the fire goes out
so does the promise

Rebirth

I shatter myself

into fractions

of my being

A pile of bones

set on fire

to produce the warmth

my life needs

A life built from ash

A phoenix reborn

Change the Future

We can smell change
we can feel it in our gut
we can see it in the wind

It presents itself
as obvious
If we don't stop to look
we will miss it

Grab it
Hold onto it
Change the future

Grow

Towering giants surround me
they move with intend
consuming only
what makes them stronger

Will I ever make it
to match their greatness?
One can aim high
and if I am cut short
I will grow again
and again
and again

Do I grow to be cut down
or do I grow in spite of it?
These giants are selection

They decide

if we grow to wear their crowns

We too can see the horizon

we too can feast on the sun

6.

Short Change Hero

Filling the Cracks

Resistance pushes into our chest
harder than ever
We desire to change the world
to support it
to make it better

Our output is our protection
and there is no space for us
but in the cracks of society

We are the silent absorbers of pain

Brothers in Arms

I hold my shield
for others to crush
To splinter into
a thousand pieces

When I drop the wreckage
my body becomes the shield
For my Brothers
behind me

I step forward

My stance widens
and I take each blow
to the chest
until I crumble to the ground

I don't need to see the outcome

of this fight

Selfhelp

You will want to fix them
You think you have the tools
but your toolbox is locked
and the key went missing
years ago

Maybe your intuition is off
Maybe fixing a problem
that doesn't exist
is effort misplaced

Maybe fixing yourself
comes first
and all you need is a hammer
and a chisel

Replaceable

The quiet push
when we sit
Softly nudging us
to get up

We are responsible
when the world falls apart
We are the glue
that holds this impossible
network together

And when we crack from
drying in the sun
we are carved out and replaced

Used Tools

The world is a furnace

A blacksmith hammer
keeps beating us
into shape

We give in

Our minds become steel
until we soften from overuse
No sharp edges

Simple

Invisible Shields

Our flesh may be torn
and healed
We were consumed
as boys

Now we prevent the world
from eating the innocent
the helpless
the children

In secret we build shields
from our wounds

Pillar

I am sorry

for being tired

My ribs collapse

from holding up this cage

I should be stronger

Maybe if I eat myself

I can gain the endurance needed

for tasks no one asked me to do

I will just stand here

in this pain

and keep

holding

Impossible Support

Another sunless morning
breaks your spirit
but you step into the cold
without complaint

Without you
the card house would collapse
It's built on uneven ground
and impossible to keep up

But only you know this
Only you stand on
broken feet

Perfect Fit

We settle for it
and it comes easy
After all we were bred to accept it
we know nothing else

Our value is our own
The price
One life
but it may support many

Now we sweat through our clothes
We chisel ourselves into cogs
that fit perfectly in the machine
No names
No fame
Just meat

Carry the World

Maybe the world is the right place
for undervalued heroes
who reluctantly create safety
exposing themselves
never being asked
stepping up in spite

Broke
Bruised
Broken

Abused to their limits
they carry the world
They are
the Short Change Heroes

7.

Food Needs Salty Tears

Do Sharks Cry?

Can you smell the ocean
It's cold
Barely alive
And the air feels like whiplash

When we stand on the cliff
We can see all of it
And none of it
Merely a reflection of the sky

But if we fan it flat
We see ourselves
So we dive in
To hide our tears

A Cry for Help

From this darkness
we can see little light
but enough to guide
a new path

A shimmer of hope

We were only taught
silent pain
now we cry out
for help

Lone Tears

Rain falls upwards
when we decide to let it
Our misery crystallizes
and tastes so good

The rest evaporates
into thin air
Our minds reset when
we let go of our tears

But tough men don't cry
Not with others

The Flow

How does one suck it up
when we are caged
behind steel bars
forged by society

We try to pull apart the metal
but only bend ourselves
So we cry when no one looks
and soon we fill the room with tears

We stand in puddles of desperation
and swim in oceans of solitude
The more we fight
the more we cry

And soon we drown in our cage

Open Heart Surgery

When we are bend

like twigs

we can withstand the pressure

because we are branches

But when we break

we break entirely

a clean snap

a done deal

an open heart

ready to be stabbed

Salt and Heat

A bland man
in a bland world
No one wants to fit in
be we all do

Good food stands out
from the rest
if it's salted properly

Cooking to perfection
takes time
and we force ourselves
to not have time

Life's Music

Another song drives a spear
into our hearts
we find ourselves in the rhythm
we find love in the voice inside

A monumental storm tears
at our rib cage
and breaks out through our eyes
We sob

An unfamiliar scent permeates the air
and the road becomes blurry
so we listen to memories
To energy for the future

Firelike

I am sure our minds
are made of tinder
One spark and
we go up in flames
And we know one thing about fire
it burns until it consumed
Everything
Its path becomes ash
It grows to its capacity
Imagine if we grew
much like that fire
but we don't burn
No
We plant seeds along our path
Creating art

Flowers at Funerals

A man's first flowers

are at his funeral

Why is it assumed

we don't like beauty?

Our eyes leak

when we see it

And when we put another Brother

in the ground

we buy flowers for the living ones

Circle of Life

How I want to be with you
die with you
a contingency plan
for our loneliness

In this world we belong together
in the next we become one
Our tears salt the ocean
our bodies feed the worms

Brothers

The silence between us
can be filled with anything

A tough man once told me
We can just sit here
Your pain is mine
and I will stand up for
your vulnerability

This world may have let you down
It may have dimmed your light
but I will not
I will fan the flames
of your existence

We can carry the weight

Together

As Brothers we can stand

and give our true selves

to the world

Epilogue

Unarmored and Unafraid

False Masks

We have gotten so good
at putting these masks on
that we are fooled by our reflections
this is who we are

The stench of our rotten flesh
under these masks is the only sign
that there was once beautiful skin
beneath them

We tear our faces off when we remove them
and we tend to the wounds
and build our scars
and once we crush the false faces

We can finally look at Ourselves in the mirror again

Reshaping Tools

Now we smelter our shattered pride
into ingots from which we form tools

Can our toolbox be too heavy?

We have garages full and need but a few
yet we keep every piece
Problems come in all shapes and sizes
we would rather be prepared
than fail before starting

Sky King Richard Russel

I hope the sky feels like it looks

A soft warm end

The sky is no limit

and the birds know this

My king lives there

Just a broken soul without screws

Freedom here on earth

Eternal in the sky

If one may dare to follow

the outcome can be different

We can subdue our desires

or end the way we wish

Oh king of the sky lead the way
and we will follow
We Fight for what is right
We Fight for your legend

The darkness may consume us
but the dim light guides
We can see if we chose
I see you oh crown bearer

Your perfect flight patterns
a sight unseen
a calm destructive voice in the heavens
May you rest in the clouds

Folded Laundry

Then she asked why I think about that now
not understanding that it was forbidden for me to
process

And I pick up my armor again
but she strips me naked
exposes my pain
and pulls my drowning body
out of the water

I gasp for air
but my stomach is filled with saltwater
I swallowed my tears for decades

Now she reaches inside
and forces me to throw up onto the floor

Bile tastes sour
but I feel light
I hate making a mess
and grab a mop to clean my emotions

My failures easily soak into the cloth of my shirt
on the ground
I grab my clothes
and throw myself into the washer with them
maybe i can drown in there

But I survive again
so i fold my laundry
and get back to work

Ready

The world You are dreaming of

is ready for You

whenever

You are

About the Author

Daniel Wirth writes poetry the way most people avoid it, direct, raw, and without looking for an exit. A research technologist based in Los Alamos, New Mexico, he lives close to the land and writes even closer to the bone. Tough Men Don't Cry is his second poetry collection.

Made in the USA
Coppell, TX
28 June 2026

83662119R00073